SWANSEA
Moments

By David Roberts

BRYNGOLD
BOOKS

First published in Great Britain in 2012
by Bryngold Books Ltd.,
100 Brynau Wood, Cimla,
Neath, South Wales SA11 3YQ.

www.bryngoldbooks.com

Typesetting, layout,
editing and design
by Bryngold Books.

ISBN 978-1-905900-29-9

**Printed and bound
in Wales by
Gomer Press,
Llandysul, Ceredigion.**

Contents

Appreciation

Many thanks to the Lord Mayor of Swansea, Councillor Dennis James, for contributing the foreword to Swansea Moments. Once again, it is a book which would not have been possible without the help and encouragement of many people, not least those who have shared their treasured photographs.

These contributions, both large and small capture a multiude of 'moments' from the city's past and allow it to be seen from a different perspective, through the eyes of those who were there, camera in hand. We are grateful for the contributions of Peter Muxworthy, Roger Green, John Wiltshire, Peter Brabham, Norman Hurford, Hugh Rees, Roger Evans, Paul Smith, Colin Riddle, Roy Kneath, Ray & Dorothy Lewis, Viv Samuel, Brian Williams, Adeline Evans, Geoff Rees, Keith Roberts, Eileen Jones, Robert Wayne Davies, Barry Griffiths, Julie Jones, Phyllis Thomas, Steve Phillips, Alan Lloyd, John Jones, Bernard Humphries, Alan Perry, Christine Rix, Clive Cockings, David and Eluned Govier, Dr Adrian Williams, Ken & Marie John, Des Jeffreys,

Gaye Mortali, Hilary Evans, Julie Cole, Jean Evans, Andrew Hinton, Anthony Owens, Dai Vaughan, The late Dennis Skanes, Alun Roper, William Bateman, Royston Morgan, Russ Thomas, Steve & Sandra McCulloch, Cerys Heath, Charlotte Barry, Steve Davies, Vivian Davies, Sarah Briggs, David & Alexandra Roe, Bill Morris, John Murphy, Gwyneth Matthews, Jim Davies, Gerald & Jean Lindenburn, John Roberts, Keith & Ann Davies, Linda & Keith Wathan, Rita Henry, Marjorie Ball, Mrs N Keevil, Rhoda E Davies, Richard & Chris Jones, the late Harry Humphries, Richard & Anne Evans and Roger Trollope.

Others without whose help the book would not have appeared include Gerald Gabb, David Beynon, John & Barbara Southard, Anthony Isaac, Neil Melbourne and Colin Scott. Finally, I must, as always, salute my wife Cheryl for her invaluable support in the publication of this and the many other books before it. Without that I am sure the task would have been far more difficult to achieve.

Share your pictures

If you have photographs of people and places in and around Swansea right up to recent times then you too, could play a part in recording the history of your area by contributing to the next Swansea nostalgia book. Please telephone 01639 643961 or e-mail david.roberts@bryngoldbooks.com to discover the ways in which you can do this. Don't be shy. We would be delighted to hear from you.
All photographs, transparencies, negatives, black and white or colour, of people, places, events, streets, buildings, schooldays and sport are considered whatever their age, subject or format. They are all promptly returned. We can also receive your pictures electronically. Meanwhile, if you have missed any of the previous 14 books then contact us now as some titles are still available.
You can also check out our website at
www.bryngoldbooks.com
for details of our other fascinating local nostalgia books.

Foreword

As many of our citizens will readily testify, Swansea is a city that is changing today more rapidly than ever before in its history. Nowhere is the evidence of that clearer and readily available than within the pages of Swansea Moments.

For 15 consecutive years David Roberts has gathered images from many people and places to provide us with a fascinating glimpse back into the past of our proud city. This book is certainly a worthy companion to all those that have been published before it and is one that all who turn its pages are sure to enjoy.

Few towns and cities across the length and breadth, not only of Wales, but the whole of the United Kingdom can boast such a comprehensive collection of images of its past, as the series David has generated on Swansea. So it is perhaps, not surprising that each new edition, of what has become an annual publication, is eagerly awaited.

Those lucky enough to be in possession of all 15 titles will have a veritable album of Swansea's growing up. Simply dipping into the pages that follow will reveal snippets of everyone's everyday lives and provide a hint to the part we all play in the history of our city by the sea.

They say a picture tells a thousand words. That sentiment is certainly true of some of those within Swansea Moments. There are images of people at work, rest and play interspersed with countless scenes of our central and suburban streets that reveal them as almost unrecognisable to those we walk or drive along today.

David often sums up his books as being, by the people, for the people. That's a modest statement, but nonetheless one that is perfectly true, for without regular contributions there would be no fresh annual book and a huge void for many in the Swansea calendar. I commend all those whose contribution is acknowledged within these pages.

More importantly I would encourage many more to do the same. But you cannot have an engine without a driver and I salute David Roberts for the passion and dedication which brings it all together and ensures his delightful books keep rolling off the press for us to enjoy. As this year's first citizen I am delighted to have the opportunity to provide a foreword to a book that will undoubtedly provide much pleasure to a great many people.

Councillor Dennis James,
Lord Mayor of the
City and County of Swansea.

About the author

David Roberts has been compiling pictorial nostalgia books for 15 years. His publications are widely acknowledged as a valuable contribution to the recording of the way people and places in the area once were.

A long-time journalist and now publisher, he worked in Swansea for nearly 30 years, witnessing at first hand many of the events and changes his compelling books depict.

The culmination of his annual picture gathering is always eagerly awaited as people clamour to add to their collection, the latest in a series of books that rank as one of the best pictorial social archives in the United Kingdom.

This is his 15th book on Swansea alongside 14 others produced on its neighbouring towns of Neath and Port Talbot. David, is married, has two grown up children, was brought up in Port Talbot and now lives in Neath.

City in the spotlight

Swansea is in the global spotlight now, more than ever before. Its successful Premier League football team has seen to that. As the eyes of the world are drawn to Wales' supreme city by the sea they focus on somewhere that is lively, vibrant and keen to embrace all things modern.

All of this would please those in the distant past whose determination to survive and succeed, led to Swansea's steady growth from settlement to city. They would surely be delighted to observe the way in which what they created has been steered onwards through time.

Snapshots of this journey touching an amazing three centuries are included in this book and provide clues as to how the Swansea we know and love today unfolded. The buildings and streets that were born out of industrial prosperity can be seen in all their glory. Alongside them, enigmatic structures that help create a specific identity.

Many of the people who walked the streets before us are featured too, having been captured on camera during many facets of their daily life. United they are a vital part of the on-going story of Wales second city.

Though the pace of change has accelerated with the passing of the years, Swansea is somewhere that still retains much character despite the ravages of wartime bombing and the march of the developers. It is an eclectic mix of all things from coast to countryside, from learning to industry, tourism to what many are proud to call home.

The exact origins of Swansea are buried in the mists of time. What is crystal clear today, is that it is a city that is building on the firm foundations of the past to stake a secure claim on the future.

**David Roberts,
September 2012.**

On the street

The tram terminus in High Street, 1903. The Cameron Hotel is on the right.

The Free Library, Alexandra Road, 1903. It had yet to acquire any neighbouring buildings.

Castle Square, not to be confused with the current Castle Square that replaced Castle Gardens, in the early 1900s. The Ben Evans building can be seen to the right. The statue is that of Henry Hussey Vivian, the first Lord Swansea and son of industrialist John Hussey Vivian.

Cradock Street, and above it, the Cambrian Institute for the Deaf and Dumb, early 1900s.

The swing bridge that carried both road and rail traffic over the River Tawe, 1903. Its operator is just visible in his cabin above the bridge which opened to allow the passage of vessels up and down the river.

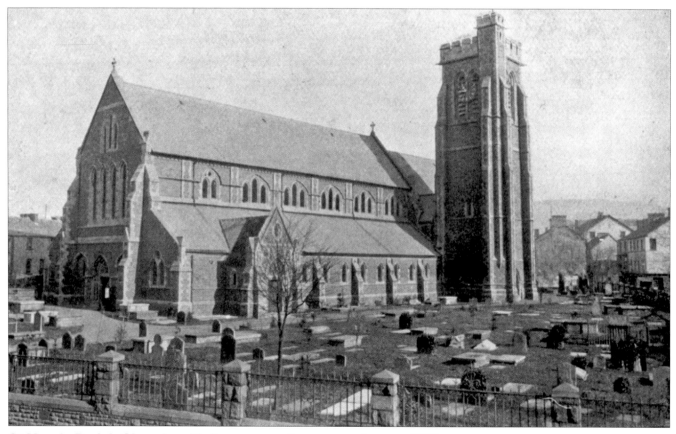

St Mary's Parish Church, with its surrounding gravestones, 1903.

A tree-lined Bryn Road near St Gabriel's Church, at its junction with Osborne Terrace, 1900. Conspicuous by their absence are the rails on which Swansea's trams would soon be running.

The Westbourne Hotel, 1, Brynymor Road, 1903. Phillips Parade is just off to the right.

This building, at 211 High Street, was home to the
Cambrian Newspaper, the South Wales Daily Post
and also the Weekly Post, 1903.

Looking along Walter Road,
towards Uplands, 1905.

Worcester Place,
looking towards
Swansea Castle
buildings, 1920s.

Retail premises in College Street, 1909. It led into Gower Street. Mount Pleasant Chapel is just visible in the background.

Pipe laying in King Edward Road, 1936. This was part of a huge city sewage scheme that linked with an outfall at Bracelet Bay.

The Bovega Restaurant, Castle Street, near its junction with Temple Street, mid-1930s. In the background is the side of the huge Ben Evans store that adjoined Temple Street.

A team of workmen hanging the Brangwyn panels, 1936.

Civic dignitaries at the official unveiling of the Brangwyn Panels at Swansea Guildhall by King George VI, 1936. The King, accompanied by Queen Elizabeth, later the Queen Mother, can be seen towards the front centre of the picture.

The foyer of the Brangwyn Hall, Swansea 1936.

Two of the British Empire Panels by Frank Brangwyn. The panel on the left is titled India, and that on the right, Canada, Industrial.

Henwood's car showroom which stood at the junction
of Oxford Street and Richardson Street, early 1950s.

The Kingsway, early 1950s. The C&A fashions store will be remembered by many.
The Plaza Cinema, later the site of the Odeon, can be seen in the distance.

This was Oxford Street, yet to recover from wartime bombing, late 1940s — twisted girders, ruins and rubble.

A view of the destruction that still remained in 1949 after Second World War bombing. The remains of Lloyd's Bank can be seen in the centre at the junction of Castle Street and Temple Street.

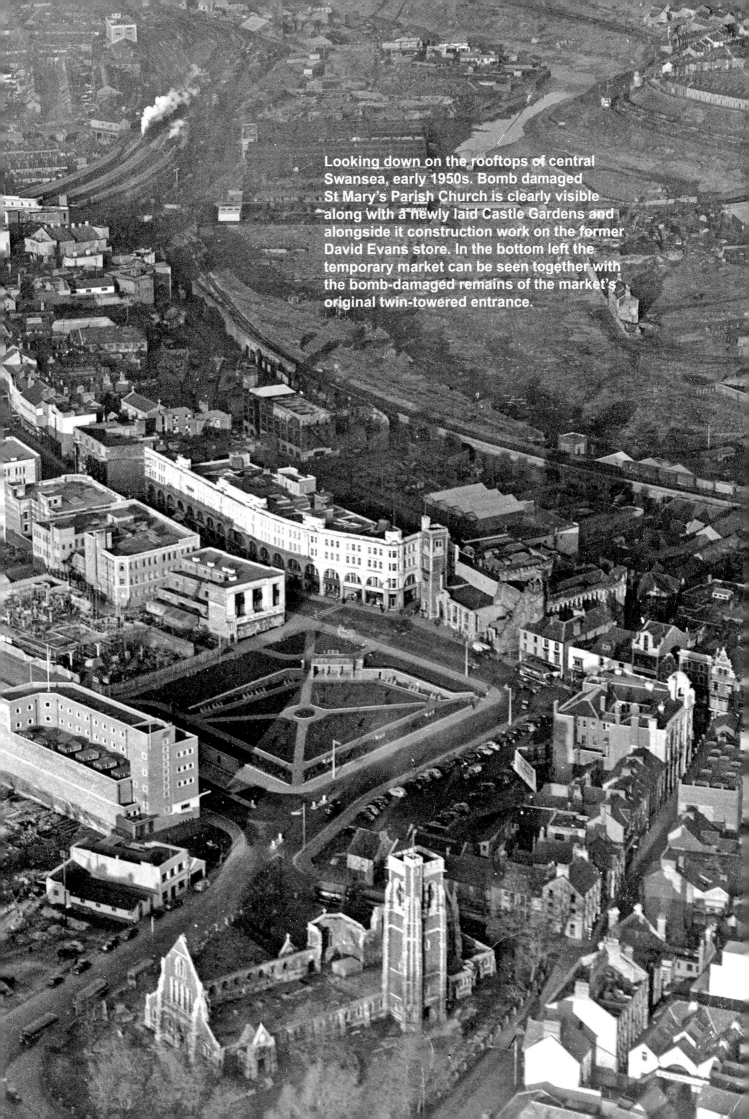

Looking down on the rooftops of central Swansea, early 1950s. Bomb damaged St Mary's Parish Church is clearly visible along with a newly laid Castle Gardens and alongside it construction work on the former David Evans store. In the bottom left the temporary market can be seen together with the bomb-damaged remains of the market's original twin-towered entrance.

The porch of the former Metropole Hotel dominates the right of this view of Wind Street, early 1950s.

The Colosseum Hotel at the junction of Wind Street and Little Wind Street, mid-1950s.

Terraces of abandoned, condemned buildings like these were commonplace in early 1960s Swansea. This was near the Vetch field.

Boots the Chemist's store, in Princess Way, was the first to be completed in Swansea's post-war rebuild. Here, in 1956, it overlooks the new Castle Gardens and on the right, the David Evans department store. Cars on the bottom left are parked on the still vacant Sidney Heath site in Caer Street.

Quay Parade was an altogether different
environment when this scene was captured on
December 12, 1959. Tank locomotive 1151 is hauling
a short train of mixed freight wagons from the main
docks on the eastern side of the River Tawe to the
South Dock area, passing Weavers Flour Mills,
now the site of Sainsbury's supermarket.

The Lewis Lewis department store was one of the shopping hotspots in High Street, 1964. It stood on the junction with King's Lane.

Traffic in St Helen's Road, near its junction with Dillwyn Street, late 1950s.

Looking seaward down Princess Way, with Castle Gardens and Caer Street on the left and the Boots store on the right, 1960. The building is now home to a McDonald's fast food restaurant. The roadway here has also been pedestrianised and absorbed by the Castle Square development.

The Mumbles train passes the forecourt of Swansea Bay station at Oystermouth Road, St Helen's, on December 12, 1959. In less than a month, on January 5, 1960, the railway closed. In the background is the landmark St Helen's rugby and cricket ground stand.

Workmen install the iconic dragon window in the Dragon Hotel, Kingsway, 1961. Below, a view of the completed building with the etched glass emblem safely in place.

This view down Constitution Hill from Terrace Road in 1975 shows why the Victorian plan to build a funicular railway was perhaps a good idea. However, operational and financial problems led to its failure.

Lower Union Street, with Peter Jones' cafe on the left and the scaffolding on the right showing post-war construction of Swansea Market, 1959.

Looking up a quiet Wind Street, 1965. Green Dragon Lane is on the right.

A giant mural of a sailing ship was one of the wonders that revealed itself in 1969 when the Metropole Hotel in Wind Street was demolished to make way for new retail development. This housed Comet and Argos, formerly Green Shield Stamps, and has itself been long demolished.

Oxford Street Secondary Modern School, shortly before demolition in 1989. The school had closed to pupils 20 years earlier in 1969. Built in 1848 it was latterly an educational resource centre.

The western end of the Quay Parade bridge over the River Tawe, Swansea's main eastern gateway, shortly before the bridge was fully opened to traffic, 1972.

Demolition of the Great Western Hotel, at the junction of High Street and Alexandra Road, is nearly complete, January 1974. It had been a grand building which curved around the junction and in the 1890s had been a Temperance hotel.

Buildings where Castle Street meets Castle Bailey Street, are overshadowed by the Post Office building of the 1850s, later home to the South Wales Evening Post for 30 years before its move to Adelaide Street in 1968. Behind that, the much higher Telecom tower in The Strand, 1976.

A panoramic view eastwards across city rooftops,
from the Guildhall clock tower, 1980.

Shoppers in
the Quadrant
Centre, 1985.

Looking across the River Tawe eastwards towards St Thomas. The building with the tall chimney on the left hand side was the ice factory, 1985.

The sad demise of Walter's Road Congregational Church, as workmen in a crane-hung cradle remove its spire, January 1988.

Shoppers throng a pedestrianised Oxford Street, 1996.

Swansea Marina, frozen over and thick with snow, viewed from Pockett's Wharf during the icy blast of January, 2010.

Scaffolding masks the Patti Pavilion as work proceeds on its refurbishment, March 19, 2008.

This was what the site of the 28-storey Meridian Tower, in Trawler Road — the tallest building in Wales — looked like on January 1, 2005. The Marriot Hotel, formerly the Holiday Inn can be seen in the background.

With the majestic sweep of the bay behind him, a unicyclist shows off his skills along the promenade, July 30, 2006.

The sign says it all. August 19, 2006 marked the end for the underpass at the Kingsway Roundabout.

Work underway on filling in the concrete bowl, once part of the Kingsway roundabout pedestrian underpass system. 2007.

Traffic congestion as work proceeds on replacing Kingsway roundabout and underpass, 2007.

Reconstruction of the roadway system at the former Kingsway roundabout, 2007.

Traffic begins to flow at the newly constructed Kingsway road junction, which replaced the roundabout and underpass, 2007.

Looking across the city centre towards the seafront, August 2, 2005. Centre stage in the background is now occupied by the Meridian Tower, in Trawler Road.

The Slip Bridge spans a Mumbles Road covered with deep snow, 1983. West Glamorgan County Hall, now Swansea Civic Centre is in the background.

Proud people

John Greaves and his bride on their wedding day, October 17, 1905. Standing between the couple is Dickie Dillwyn who became landlord of the Dillwyn Arms, Brynhyfryd Square in 1907.

Mr & Mrs Stanley Bellinger outside St Mary's Church, after their wedding, 1916.

Members of the Davey family from Hafod, early 1920s.

Some of the residents of
Langland Convalescent
Home, May 24, 1927.

A group of neighbours at
Llewellyn Circle, Mayhill,
late 1920s.

A family of itinerant travellers with their horse-drawn caravans, in Gower, 1953.

A wedding group outside St Michael's Church, Manselton, after the wedding of Roy Evans and Jean Cooling of Cecil Street, Manselton, March 1952.

Two women relax in the sunshine on a bench at Manselton Park, 1948.

Swansea and district motor traders at a dinner and dance attended by the Mayor and Mayoress, 1948.

A mother and her children with a box of kittens at No. 2 site, Fairwood, near the Devil's Elbow bend, mid-1950s.

Members of the youth club held at Cila School, 1950.

Guests at the annual Christmas dinner and dance of the St Benedict's Church, Sketty, branch of the Catholic Women's League, 1955.

Choir practice at St Paul's Church, Sketty, 1951.

Members of the 1st Swansea YMCA and Penllergaer Scout troops with 1st Swansea Scoutmaster David Vaughan at a summer camp in Cornwall in 1962. Behind them is the trusty coach used by the 1st Swansea troop on their travels for many years.

A group of office staff from Unigate Dairies, Hafod with friends, during a dinner dance at the Dolphin Hotel, 1966.

A group of friends share a pint of beer at the Eagle Inn, Treboeth, mid-1960s.

Harry Secombe greeted by his brother after arriving at Swansea Airport late 1960s.

Gors Avenue Pensioners Club, Townhill, early 1970s.

Swansea in Bloom winners with the awards they received from the Lord Mayor and Lady Mayoress, 1983.

A group of employees at a presentation ceremony at Swansea Docks with its manager,
William King, 1980.

Some of the women who prepared refreshments for the official opening of Dunvant Rugby Club.

Office staff of Unigate dairies during a presentation at the company's Cwmdu depot, 1992.

Members of Mumbles Community Council with the Archbishop of Canterbury, Dr Rowan Williams, during a visit he made to Oystermouth Castle, 2002.

Suburban scenes

Children play in the roadway
at Bonymaen, 1905.

St Thomas viewed from Townhill, 1893. St Thomas School is a recognisable landmark. Alexandra Road can be seen bottom right, pointing towards High Street station.

Sketty Cross, 1905. The Vivian Arms is on the left and across the road below it, the Bush Inn. Horse power was still the main form of transport then.

The road through Bonymaen was much quieter in 1911. According to the sign across the front of the Bonymaen Inn, the premises served up Hancock's unrivalled ales and stout.

Looking up Clase Road, Morriston Cross, mid-1920s.

Postmen and staff outside Gorseinon Post Office, 1910.

Children at play in Primrose Park, Llansamlet, 1910.

Uplands Square, looking towards Gower Road, 1924. The Uplands Hotel is in the distance.

Mr and Mrs Evan John Smith, feeding the chickens in the garden of their home at Lamberts Cottages, Swansea Docks, 1929.

Edith, Aubrey and Lettie Daniel at the gateway of their home, No. 5 Gorwydd Terrace, Waunarlwydd, 1930.

Hendrefoilan House, Killay, now part of Swansea University, 1930.

Dyfed Avenue, Townhill, 1950.

Looking towards Gower Road, across Pwll Mawr, Upper Killay, 1950.

Looking westwards across Swansea rooftops towards Townhill, 1930s. The Teacher Training College Is In the dIstance.

Shops at The Square, Killay, 1934. To the right is the Black Boy public house.

Ravenhill Park in the icy grip of the long, cold winter of 1947.

The view across Swansea Bay towards Mumbles Head, from Cwmgwyn, Sketty, late 1950s.

The old hall at Upper Killay. At one time, following the Second World War it was used regularly for dances and film shows. It was also used as a baby clinic in the early 1950s.

Gower Road, Killay, 1954. The Railway Inn is among the trees on the left.

Buildings at Gower Road, Upper Killay which were home to machinery and engineering company Greenings, 1955. This is now the site of the Mike Davies Camping and Leisure premises.

New shops at Broadmead, Killay at what was known as the Buildahome estate. The shopping centre opened on October 2, 1962.

Construction work underway on Quay Parade, early 1960s. The tall building in the centre is Hancock's brewery.

The road beneath this railway bridge at Port Tennant is being lowered and widened, to accomodate the coming of the new Fabian Way dual carriageway, early 1960s.

Road widening between Cwmdu and Mile End, Carmarthen Road, Fforestfach, 1991.

A polling station at Sketty Green, April 9, 1992.

A nightime view of Alexandra Road and Dyfatty flats from the roof of Swansea College of Art, November 5,1965.

The boating lake and restaurant at Singleton Park, late 1970s.

It was a case of bottoms up for these ducks at Brynmill Park lake, April 1966.

The Swiss Chalet and adjoining cafe at Singleton Park, late 1960s.

The newly built Liberty Stadium, and behind, Swansea Enterprise Park, August 2, 2005.

Construction of the new road bridge over the River Loughor, mid-1980s.

Shopping days

The well stocked glass, china and earthenware stall of E Britton at Swansea Market. 1887.

Clinton P Scott, grocer, tea dealer and provision merchant with customers outside his shop at No. 7 St Helen's Road, 1903.

The piano and organ shop of J Brader and Sons, 9 Wind Street, 1903.

Olga, a 14 year old girl serving at a fruiterers stall in Swansea market, 1909.

Moore Bros, grocers and provision merchants, Crown Stores, St Helen's Road, 1903.

Staff outside a David Evans store of the early 1900s.

Penclawdd cockle women selling their wares at Swansea Market, late 1920s.

The opening day of two new shops at the Square, Llansamlet, 1912. On the left is the butchery of A Thomas and alongside, Llansamlet Post Office.

The cycle and motor shop of Dan Morgan Ltd, 57 Oxford Street, 1903.

The bakery and grocery shop of TJ Rice at Gower Road, Sketty, early 1950s.

Checking out the produce at Macfisheries store, Portland Street, 1960.

The High Street store of FW Woolworth, the 3d and 6d store, long before the days of pound shops, complete with its popular first floor cafeteria, mid-1950s.

The Llangyfelach Road store of Swansea Teleservices, now a house. Outside, owner and proprietor John Feldman, 1997.

The Glanyrafon Stores of J Evans & Company at 815 Carmarthen Road, Fforestfach, late 1950s. The property was eventually demolished to make way for a road widening scheme.

Arthur Llewellyn Jenkins furniture store, Neath Road, Plasmarl, 1976.

Shops at Sketty Cross, mid-1960s.

Plasmarl Post Office, 1969.

Produce from the surrounding countryside on sale at Swansea's popular market, 1969.

Special occasions

Elephants lead the way as a circus parade passes along Victoria Road, 1905. The gabled building was the Sailors' Rest, later the first Swansea Dockers' Club.

A horse drawn carnival float with a political theme, early 1900s.

The East Side carnival queen with her attendants, 1933.

All dressed up and ready to participate in East Side carnival, 1935.

Celebrating the end of the Second World War at Fleet Street, Sandfields, 1945.

Residents of Fleet Street during VE Day celebrations, 1945.

The commandos of Broughton Bay, a group of entrants in Llangennith Carnival, 1955. They won a special extra prize of 10 shillings (50p) for originality.

Residents of Lon Cedwyn, Sketty, during a street party held to mark VE Day, 1945.

Participants in a procession which took place on the re-opening of St Mary's Church in 1959.
It started at St James's Church in Walter Road and walked down through the town.

During the late 1950s and early 1960s, the Metallurgy Department at Swansea University always had a float in its annual Rag Week procession. It was often based on a set of old cart wheels. Following the procession, the float was burned on the university site. This stagecoach is seen leaving the site to join a procession around 1960.

A syndicate of South Wales Transport fitters at the company's Ravenhill depot who had a bumper win on the football pools, 1960.

A street party in Dillwyn Road, Sketty, to celebrate the Coronation of Queen Elizabeth II, June, 1953.

Sebastopol Street, St Thomas, decorated with bunting to celebrate the Investiture of the Prince of Wales, July, 1969.

The Swansea College of Technology float that was entered in the city's Rag Week procession, 1962.

Two women rattle their collecting tins for charity at Penlan Carnival, 1976.

Part of the parade at Mumbles Carnival, 1967.

One of the floats that took part in Bishopston Carnival, 1992.

Churchgoers carry a wooden
cross to the top of Kilvey Hill as
part of a Good Friday procession
of witness, mid-1970s.

Swansea superstar Catherine Zeta Jones and fellow Welsh entertainer Stan Stennett, who was
brought up in Gorseinon, during a party organised by members of the Swansea branch of the
Motor Neurone Society, 1990.

Her Majesty Queen Elizabeth II in the forecourt of High Street railway station during her visit to the city as part of her Silver Jubilee celebration tour, 1977.

Led by two regimental goat mascots, a contingent of Welsh Guards passes Swansea Guildhall during a ceremonial parade to celebrate being granted the freedom of the city, 1979.

SWANSEA
Moments

The young ones

Members of the 4th Swansea, Sketty Baptist Scout troop, at camp in Parc-le-Breos, Parkmill, Whitsun 1940. This was the weekend of the German invasion of Belgium, Luxembourg and The Netherlands and as a result the camp broke up a day early.

A young brother and sister with their mum at 41 Cambridge Street, Uplands, 1947.

Pupils of Christ Church School, Oystermouth Road, during a Nativity play, 1947.

Brothers and sisters of the Dempster family in the back garden of their home at Rock Street, off Lion Street, Waun Wen, 1949.

The junior carnival queen and attendants at East Side carnival, 1936.

A youngster receives a gift from Father Christmas at Leslie's High Street store, 1951.

Young love in action. It started with a kiss, in Bath Road, Morriston, 1953.

Two young girls from Sea View Terrace, North Hill, on the back of a relative's motorcycle, 1950.

Young children at William Street, during celebrations of the Coronation of Queen Elizabeth II, 1953.

Members of the second Mumbles, Swansea Brownie pack with Brown Owl Gwen Hopkins, in Underhill Park near the loft where they held their meetings, June 1951.

Officers and members of Swansea 215 Squadron ATC, 1952.

Pantygwydr Brownies, Uplands, during a Nativity play, 1955.

Members of the Band of Hope group at Hermon Chapel, Plasmarl, all set for a performance of the pantomime Snow White and the Seven Dwarves, mid-1950s.

Two young girls, resplendant in their traditional Welsh costume at William Street on St David's Day, 1957. The perimeter wall of the now vanished Vetch Field can be seen in the background.

Young members of the congregation of St Phillip's Church, Bathurst Street, Sandfields, during their Christmas party, 1961.

A group of Bishopston Scouts and Cubs take their promise, 1997.

Pupils of Martin Street Junior Boys' School stage a Christmas play at the Forward Movement Hall, Woodfield Street, Morriston 1958.

Participants in a Nativity play at Einon Church, Morriston, 1956.

Youngsters enjoy a ride on a miniature steam powered railway at Derwen Fawr, May 1985.

The cast of Penlan Comprehensive School's production of Oliver with civic visitors, West Glamorgan County Councillor Tom Jones and his wife Doreen, 1989.

Some of the male members of the cast of Pentrehafod School's successful production of the musical Grease in 1996.

Lesson time

A class at St Helen's Girls' School 1928.

Pupils of class 5 at Cila School, 1920.

Class 1A, Graig School, 1923.

The 'Babies' B class of Oxford Street Infants School, 1911.

Pupils of class 9 at St Helen's Junior School, Brynmill, 1936.

Class 1, Brynhyfryd School, 1954.

Pupils at Sketty Infants School, with their teacher and headteacher, 1960.

Pupils at Gors Junior School, during their Harvest Festival, 1948.

Form 5B Dynevor School, autumn 1957 with teachers Horace Griffiths, left and R Harries, right and headteacher Meredydd Hughes.

Pupils and teachers of Llanmorlais School, celebrate around the maypole, perhaps to commemorate the 1937 Coronation.

Some of the teachers and pupils of Mynyddbach Secondary School for Girls, in September 1960, the year it opened.

Class J4, Parklands School, Sketty, 1963.

Mynyddbach Girls' School prefects, 1965.

Seated with their headteacher and teacher is a class of girl pupils at Cefn Hengoed School, Winch Wen, 1967 — the year it opened.

Pupils of form 2D, Llansamlet Comprehensive School, with their teacher, 1980.

St David's Day celebrations at Pentrepoeth Infants School, 1973.

Class 8 at St Joseph's Roman Catholic Junior School, Greenhill, with teacher Mrs Reagan, 1981.

Form 2E, Bishop Vaughan Comprehensive School, 1981.

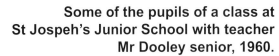

Some of the pupils of a class at
St Jospeh's Junior School with teacher
Mr Dooley senior, 1960.

Pupils of form 3Y, Morriston Senior Comprehensive School, 1981.

119

A class of pupils at St Joseph's RC Junior School, Greenhill, with their teacher David Alexander, 1982.

Pupils of Martin Street Junior
Boys School, Morriston, 1985.

Class 3, Brynhyfryd Junior School,
with teacher David Lewis, 1983.

This was the last day at Graig Infants School, Morriston, for these pupils who were set to move to the junior school, July 19, 1983. Sadly, Graig Infants School closed in the summer of 2012.

In their lines before the start of lessons are these pupils of Graig Infants School, Morriston, July 19, 1983.

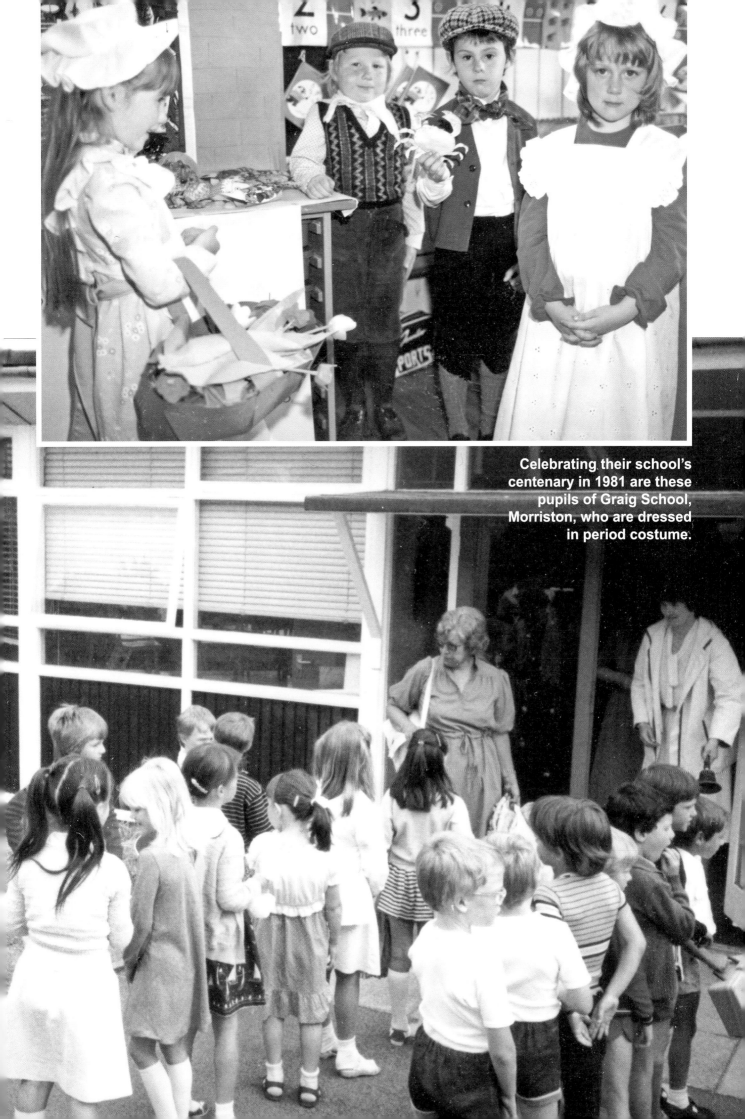

Celebrating their school's centenary in 1981 are these pupils of Graig School, Morriston, who are dressed in period costume.

Youngsters of Cwmrhydyceirw Primary School, Morriston, July 10, 2006.

The reception class at Cwmrhydyceirw Primary School, Morriston, 1996.

Moving methods

A traction engine operated by Greening & Sons of Upper Killay, hauls a huge transformer to Swansea Corporation's power station in The Strand, 1920s.

A tradesman with his pony and trap, early 1900s.

A group of motorcycle combination riders prepare to set off for Mumbles and Oxwich from Swansea with passengers who consisted mainly of wounded ex-servicemen, pre-1920. Their machines are mainly of Royal Enfield make.

A traction engine owned by Greening & Sons, Upper Killay, hauling logs, early 1900s. The company operated machinery and were also timber merchants.

A cyclist shows off his prowess in Swansea town centre, 1920.

A steam hauled Mumbles train arrives at Southend, mid-1920s. Judging by the crowds at the waters edge this was Regatta Day.

This charabanc operated by E Harries & Sons appears to be ready to take its passengers on a day trip. It is pictured in Woodfield Street, Morriston, early 1920s.

An early South Wales Transport AEC open top double decker bus prepares to leave for Mumbles from the town centre, late 1920s.

A group of motorcyclists prepares to set off on a run from Oxford Street, late 1920s.

A steam powered wagon and trailer operated by Greening & Sons of Upper Killay, late 1920s.

Two trams at Eversley Road, Sketty, 1936.

Looking north east along Eversley Road from Sketty tram terminus, mid-1930s.

The premises of the Sketty Motor Company, a partnership between Messrs Thomas and Joslyn, early transport operators along Gower routes, in the 1920s.

An early standard car pictured at the side of Mumbles Road, early 1930s.

Two of the vehicles operated by South Wales Auto Electrical Services, mid-1950s.

This is how the milk was brought to Mumbles from Upper Killay in the 1930s. David and Martha Morris had a round linking the two districts for many years.

Swansea tram car No 43 at Eversley Road, Sketty, 1930s.

Established in 1908 this was one of the removal lorries used by Henwood's Removals, early 1950s.

One of the tipper trucks used by the South Wales Sand & Gravel Company in the early 1950s.

Locomotives at Paxton Street engine shed on May 17, 1959.

A loading machine fills a tipper lorry operated by the South Wales Sand & Gravel Company, early 1950s. The work was possibly during removal of Pentrehafod tip.

Three locomotives appear to be rounding up an errant flock of sheep that escaped onto the railway line in the lower Clyne Valley, near Mumbles Road station, mid-1950s.

Passengers board a train to Mumbles at Rutland Street, 1959. Hancock's brewery can be seen in the background.

An AEC Bridgemaster double decker bus bound for Clase, picks up passengers in Orchard Street in 1961. In the background, construction of the Dragon Hotel is nearing completion.

A standard class British Railways locomotive, No. 80097 passes Swansea Beach at The Slip on a summer's day in 1963 as it hauls a two-carriage local train to Pontarddulais. The Bay View Hotel is in the background.

The Scillonian, purchased by P&A Campbell's White Funnel Fleet arriving at Swansea on a high tide early evening, May 1977.

City Minis, which carried people in and out of Swansea from the districts form the nucleus of vehicles in attendance at the Quadrant Shopping Centre Bus Station, mid-1980s.

The Swansea to Cork Ferry passing rocks at Bracelet Bay, on its way into its city berth, mid-1990s.

Taking a break

A family prepares for a train journey from the Midland Railway station, Morriston, early 1900s.

A Swansea family enjoys a donkey cart trip during a holiday in Ireland, 1945.

A group of Hafod residents pose for the camera during a day out at Windsor, mid-1920s.

A family enjoys some time in the sun at Swansea Sands, near the Slip bridge, 1949.

A group of Swansea people alongside the coach that took them on a day trip to Fishguard, 1953.

Members of the South Wales Transport Company's Magnet Club prepare to set off on an outing in the early 1960s — on one of the company's coaches of course!

A group of female members of staff from the High Street department store of Lewis Lewis, during a staff outing to Tenby, June 1954. The trip was attended by most of the staff of the various departments situated on the store's ground floor.

Girls from Llwyn Y Bryn School make friends with a local village girl in Switzerland on a trip to Venice, 1956.

This group is taking a break from one of the Youth for Christ rallies held at Mount Pleasant Baptist Church, The Kingsway, in the late 1950s and attended by visiting evangelists.

Members of the Men's Guild of Terrace Road Chapel, Mount Pleasant, on the Cake Walk ride at Coney Beach funfair during an outing to Porthcawl, 1959.

Youngsters enjoy
some fun in the sand
at Caswell,
early 1980s.

A group of regulars at the Eagle Inn, Treboeth, all set to head off on a trip to Ireland, 1969.

Members of Dunvant Male Choir assembled at the Brangwyn Hall, before setting off for their 1995 centenary tour to America and Canada. The tour saw them give six official concerts. Centrally in the front are Arwyn Walters, musical director; Dennis Rees, chairman; Mrs Peggy Morgan, president; Allan Fewster, accompanist and Roger Clegg, assistant accompanist.

A solitary stroller on Swansea sands, August 1967.

On the beach at Oxwich, Gower, June, 1968.

The rescue operation at its height after the grounding of the pleasure vessel Prince Ivanhoe, at Porteynon, Gower, on August 3, 1981.

Pentrehafod School choir and orchestra on a successful visit to Paris in July 2005. The musicians, under the direction of Mrs Carter, gave two concerts in the city, including one in Parc Du Luxemburg.

SWANSEA
Moments

Off to work

A threshing machine at work in a field at Manselfield, Murton, early 1900s.

A group of Gower farm workers alongside a fully laden hay cart, early 1900s.

Agricultural workers used an N D Greenings threshing machine at Manselfield, Murton, 1920s.

A traction engine and its crew, tree felling in Killay, early 1920s.

The Second World War rescue team at the RTZ company's Swansea Vale Works, Llansamlet. Sitting with the cup is Bill Reason of Skewen who later became general manager of the works.

Employees of the Elba Tinplate Works, Crymlyn Burrows, 1929.

Members of the National Fire Service at Swansea, during the Second World War, 1942.

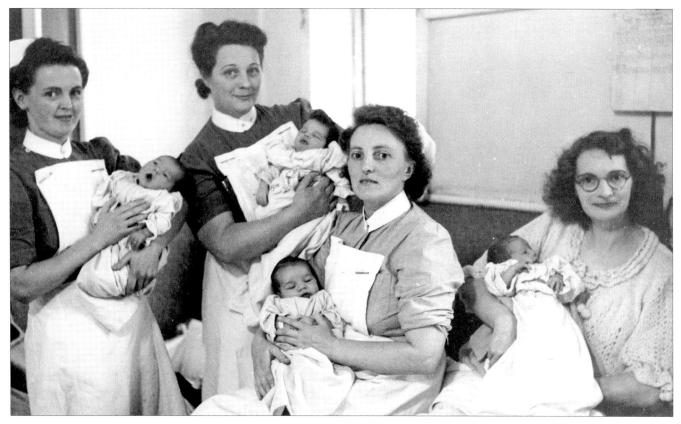

Midwives and a proud mum with babies born at Fairwood Hospital, on September 6, 1948.

A group of employees at National Benzole fuel company's distribution depot, just off Morriston Common, in front of one of the company's road tankers, mid-1950s.

Young railwaymen at Paxton Street locomotive depot, Sandfields, 1956.

Cockle gatherers with their ponies and traps on the sands at Penclawdd, mid-1950s.

Staff behind the counter of the Welsh Dry Cleaners shop, 96 Brynymor Road, early 1960s.

Some of the men, employed by R M Douglas Construction, who helped build Trostre steelworks, Llanelli, 1952.

Employees at work in the Milton Taylor engineering company at Weig Fach Lane, Fforestfach, 1960. Founded in 1948 the company specialised in the reconditioning of gas cylinder valves for Calor Gas and other bottled gas suppliers. The building, now a housing estate, was originally the command post and plotting room for the fighter station at RAF Fairwood during the Second World War. The company continues to operate as RMS Gas Engineering Ltd, in Gorseinon.

Staff of Marks & Spencer's Oxford Street store during a presentation, 1960.

Teaching staff at Arfryn Primary School, 1978.

Staff at Swansea
Garden Centre,
Blackpill, take a
break, mid-1970s.

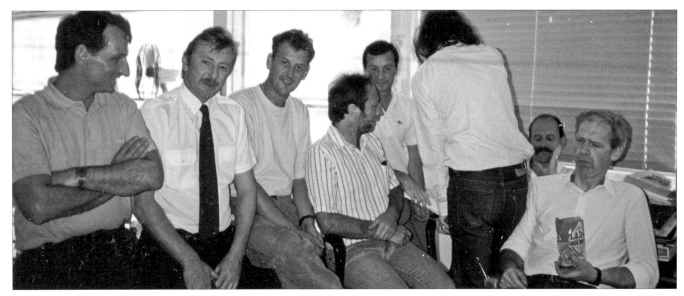

BT Swansea engineering control staff taking a break from office duties at their Strand HQ, 1989.

Non-teaching staff at Mynyddbach Girls' School, mid-1990s.

Staff of Cefn Hengoed School, Winch Wen, 2005.

Mumbles & Gower

Langland Bay, mid-1860s.

A view across Mumbles, around 1930.

The Porteynon lifeboat, Janet, which served the area from 1906-1916. It is being hauled ashore by a team of horses.

A packed day at Mumbles Pier, early 1900s.

An interesting perspective of Mumbles Pier shortly before the arrival of one of the popular pleasure steamers that called there to pick up and drop off passengers, 1911.

Mount Hermon Chapel, Penclawdd, built in 1807 and pictured in the early 1900s.

Looking across Langland Bay, 1925. Lined up along the beach is a row of bathing huts.

One of the wooden bungalows at Limeslade, 1923. It was the second built in the area by Stanley Hinton who is seen on the left. His wife and other relatives are also present. Somerset House, which still stands today on Mumbles Hill can be seen at the top left.

Work underway at Oystermouth station on the Mumbles main drainage scheme, 1936.

The drainage scheme outfall at Mumbles Head, nears completion, 1936.

Boats laid up alongside the Mumbles Railway at Southend, 1959.

Mumbles Head and Bracelet Bay, 1963.

Mumbles viewed from Oystermouth Castle, August 1964.

Ponies, cows and motorists mingle at Ryers Down, Gower, 1965.

Pleasure craft moored at Mumbles, mid-1960s.

The old Church at Llanmadoc, May 1967.

Knab Rock, Mumbles, late 1960s.

A flock of sheep impedes the flow of traffic on the North Gower Road, August 1972.

Dick Barton's fish & chip restaurant, 2008. For decades it has been the rendezvous for hungry hordes at West Cross.

Looking up Castle Avenue, off Newton Road, Mumbles, towards Oystermouth Castle. 1988.

A team effort

Bowls players at a tournament at Cwmdonkin Park, 1926.

Members and supporters of Morriston Hockey Team, 1927.

Members of Morriston tennis team, 1939.

Tennis Courts at Cwmdonkin Park, late 1930s.

The Welsh Schools' Football Association team that played Ireland, 1948.

A womens' football team at Killay, with the spoils of a successful encounter, mid-1950s.

Swansea Town who were Division 3 (South) Champions, 1953.

Penlan Multilateral School Senior B football team, 1957.

Former landlord of the Brynmelyn Arms, Dick Bradley, with friends in O'Connell Street, Dublin where they had gone to spectate at a rugby international which Wales duly won, 1950. On their flight home the aircraft carrying them crashed in fog on its approach to Llandow Airfield. In total 75 passengers and five crew members died in the disaster. It was, at the time, the worst accident in British aviation history. Three passengers survived, among them former WRU president Handel Rogers.

Penlan School B football team, Swansea Schools' league champions, 1956-57.

St Augustine's AFC, 1948-49 season.

The rugby team at Grange School, West Cross, with their teacher and headteacher in 1953, the year they became Swansea Junior Schools League champions.

Members of Penlan Multilateral School's Arthur house team, school boxing champions 1958.

Fairwood Rangers football team, with their captain proudly displaying the spoils of a successful season, late 1950s.

With plenty of trophies to prove it, these men were members of the Magnet Club Darts team which won the Morriston Hospital Darts League, 1964.

Bishop Gore's Swansea Grammar School, 2nd XV, 1955-6.

Morriston Hospital Darts League committee and players at the league's annual presentation evening, 1969.

Receiving their trophies are the winners of the womens' doubles competition in the Swansea Spastics Darts League tournament, 1967. With them is Albert Athernought, chairman of the league.

Two successful competitors in the Rotherslade to Langland swim, 1967. They were both members of Neath Swimming Club.

Trophy winners in the Swansea Spastics Darts League at the Magnet Club, 1968.

A lone hang glider soars off the down at Rhossili, July 24, 1979.

Swansea's It's a Knockout team members representing GB in Maastricht as UK champions, 1975.

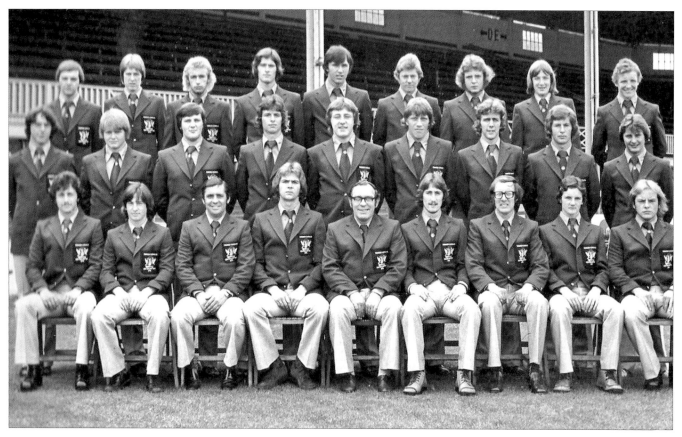

Members of the Swansea Schools' Rugby Union Squad which toured New Zealand, 1976.

Pentrehafod School soccer team with coach Geoff Rees. The team reached the final of the Urdd (Youth) soccer competition, 1979.

Fathers of St Joseph's School football team players who competed against the fathers of a visiting German team at Morfa Stadium, April 27, 1985.

Boxer Colin Jones is mobbed by fans as he arrives home at High Street station after winning the Commonwealth and European championship, 1981.

The football squad of Martin Street Junior School, Morriston, with their teacher-trainer, 1985.

Footballing legend John Toshack with the winners of a charity football match between the men and the women of Unigate Dairies, Swansea, 1984.

Competitors line up for the massed start of the Swansea Bay 10k run
alongside St Helen's Sports ground on Oystermouth Road, 2009.
Inset, entrants can be seen pounding their way along the foreshore route.

Casllwchwr Junior School soccer
team with teacher Mr Jones, 1992.

Swansea Schools' Cricket
Association senior squads
and officers before a
game at Ashleigh Road
playing fields, 1982.

West Indies cricket captain, Viv Richards shakes hands with a Swansea spectator after his side played Glamorgan at St Helen's on July 13, 14, 15, 1988.

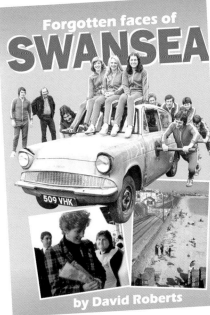
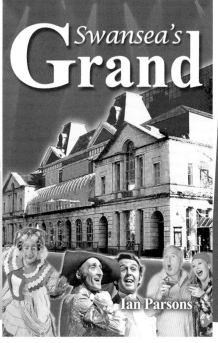
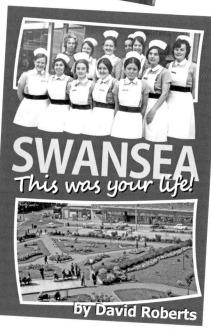
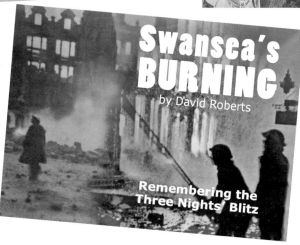
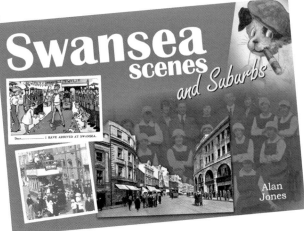